MW00773638

The Successful Mortgage Broker

DISCLOSURE

This publication contains the opinions and ideas of its authors. It is sold with the understanding that the authors and publisher are not engaged in rendering legal, accounting, investment or other professional services. Laws vary from state to state and federal laws may apply to a particular transaction, and if the reader requires expert financial or other assistance or legal advice, a competent professional should be consulted. Neither the authors nor the publisher can guarantee the accuracy of the information contained herein.

The authors and publisher specifically disclaim any responsibility for any liability, loss or risk, personally or otherwise, which is incurred as a consequence, directly or indirectly, of the use and application of any of the contents of this book.

The Successful Mortgage Broker

Selling Mortgages After the Meltdown

JASON C. MYERS

WITH MICHAEL SHANNON II

WWW.PALMETTOPUBLISHINGGROUP.COM

Palmetto Publishing Group, LLC
Charleston, SC

Products, pictures, trademarks, and trademarked names are used throughout this book to describe various proprietary products that are owned by third parties. No endorsements of the information contained in this book is given by the owners of such products and trademarks, and no endorsement is implied by the inclusion of product, pictures, or trademarks in this book.

Copyright © 2015 Jason C. Myers & Michael Shannon II
All rights reserved. No portion of this book may be reproduced, stored in a retrieval system, or transmitted in any form by any means–electronic, mechanical, photocopy, recording, or other–except for brief quotations in printed reviews, without prior permission of the publisher.

For more information regarding special discounts for bulk purchases, please contact Palmetto Publishing Group at Info@PalmettoPublishingGroup.com.

ISBN-13: 978-1944313029
ISBN-10: 1944313028

Table of Contents

1

Introduction – Where We Came From

As a whole, the mortgage industry is exactly like the Wild West, both currently and in its recent past. We've gone from an outlaw nation with very little in the way of rules, to an industry dominated by ultimate penalties. In today's world of mortgages, we face more regulations than ever before in history, resulting in loan officers facing a lynch-mob mentality, much like would have been seen during the days of Billy the Kid. The level of fines, costs, compliance and overall increase of government control are pushing the mortgage broker to the brink of extinction. Much like the Wild West of old, it seems as if the penalties are designed to eliminate the outlaws. I equate them to hanging offenses nowadays, and in my opinion, they have gone *a little too far*. My goal in writing this book is to put some ideas and dialogue in place to help others like me do one thing: Survive and succeed in the face of these current industry hurdles.

It is impossible to understand the breadth of what we face as brokers today without understanding where we came from and what we faced as an industry. I will relay my share of a story, already told by numerous others, from my perspective as a broker operating since roughly mid-2003. I've been a basic mortgage broker, a banker (briefly), a manager of a small shop, and the owner of a company listed on the Inc. 5000, a list of the fastest-growing private companies in the nation, in 2012 and 2013. Along the way, I've learned numerous lessons I hope to share with the goal of helping more brokers be successful while avoiding some of the mistakes I've made.

Additionally, I think I have a unique perspective since my first job out of college was in another heavily regulated industry, working as a financial advisor for Merrill Lynch in Charleston, South Carolina. To obtain that position, I was required to pass the Series 7, Series 66, and state insurance licensing exams. I was given almost eight months to study and prep, while receiving a small base salary of roughly $2,000 a month. As I was straight out of college with a finance degree, this was a good gig and gave me the first real taste of regulations and how they would affect me throughout my career.

I clearly see the parallels between the level of testing and licensing rules being put in place and where I think the regulators want to take the industry. The fact that loan officers cannot contact clients until after they pass their exams is one clear example. Once I passed the required tests, I was given the green light to go earn my keep, which essentially meant cold calling and lots of lunches spent trying to impress people with more wealth than I, all while being roughly the same age as most of their children at a young twenty-two years old.

After approximately two years with Merrill Lynch, I found out the hard way how significantly regulations—in this case, corporate regulations—could affect a person's life. I made the mistake of sending an email with some rather colorful language to a coworker, who in turn thought it would be funny to teach the new guy a lesson by showing it to our compliance officer—who promptly showed the head man, who promptly fired me. And just like that, I'd discovered that sending an email talking in detail about taking a dump on the boss's desk was a quick way to be escorted from the building. Next thing you know, I was on my way to becoming a mortgage broker. . . .

In 2003, when I first answered a job ad from a local mortgage brokerage company, I was essentially asked two things: Had I ever committed a felony involving a financial instrument? And could I pay the $75 licensing fee to the South Carolina Department of Consumer Affairs?

I answered both of these questions correctly, passed a simple background check, and within a week was ready to start selling. So, in comparison, we went from waiting eight months to get the Security and Exchange Commission (SEC) green light to play ball to a short week-long process before getting to smiling and dialing. Mortgage brokerage regulations are clearly pushing us to something similar. Not as difficult, but comparable.

Needless to say, after being trained by Merrill Lynch to work with a system consisting of dialing a hundred random strangers a day, going to a system where we called leads obtained online or from local referral sources caused me to become quite successful very early. Within a year or so, a regional bank offered me a position and my very first signing bonus. I gladly accepted! A very short six months later, I was ready to blow up the bank and swore I'd never again work in an environment I couldn't control. Fortunately, I was offered a position by my previous employer, along with a raise and a promotion to manager of a new location in Mount Pleasant, South Carolina.

It was in this position that I started to gain knowledge and developed my ability to help others in our industry grow and sell. I helped quickly build our branch to become the most successful in the company, hiring and growing a team along the way.

Around this time, the industry as a whole seemed to lose its mind, and the products that came with it led to calamity in 2008. I will be the first to say that we sold the products we were given and in some cases scratched our heads at the results. I sold plenty of option adjustable-rate mortgages (ARMs) to many investors and high net worth individuals for Washington Mutual and Indy Mac Loan. I refused to sell the 100 Percent Financing Bear Stearns No-Doc Option ARM, a product that scared me with the unbelievable stupidity of its concept. I remember the account representative saying that while they had a low negative amortization (NegAm) loan on the first mortgage, Bear Stearns was going to make a killing on the fixed-rate second mortgages at 13 percent interest.

To clarify for those not from our world at that time and previously, NegAm loans were based on a low teaser rate that allowed the consumer to buy property with 20 percent down and then use that equity like a credit card, with the monthly payment not covering the total interest cost. NegAm loans were created because of the runaway housing market, during which values always went up—right? Back to Bear Stearns: These geniuses decided, "To hell with having some equity and collateral to work with! Let's create a product where the borrower can go with an option ARM or negative amortization on the first mortgage to 80 percent; then we'll lend them the other 20 percent on a fixed-rate mortgage at 13 to 15 percent interest. Oh, and by the way, let's also do this as a no-doc loan," which means all they did was a credit check to make sure applicants had at least a 620 credit score and boom, that would give them financing.

It was then that I realized our industry was seriously screwed because someone way above me had lost his or her freaking mind. There I was, roughly twenty-seven years old, and I could see that this product line had doom and bad intentions written all over it. That one product led me to discover that things would get bad and eventually end bad. Bear Stearns honestly thought it was good that they got to keep the fixed-rate second mortgage.

Think logically for a second: You're giving a borrower with a low credit score a loan working in reverse—remember the whole concept is that the balance increases on the first lien. Keep in mind this is 100 percent financing, meaning those lower-end borrowers had no skin in the game. They literally had no money in the transaction except for maybe paying some closing costs. These geniuses let a loan heading backward in the first-lien position in front of their more expensive fixed-rate second mortgages. So when things went bad, what do you think they quit paying? Knowing that they were already unqualified for the first mortgage, do you really think they gave a rat's ass about paying the 13-percent second mortgage? Which meant, by the way, those in the second-lien position were essentially out of money when the home values crashed. This wasn't just a bad product—it was an *idiotic product*.

About the same time as the aforementioned financial meltdown, a group of us left our current employers and started out on our own. We formed a small lending group on borrowed furniture with a processor who dropped everything and moved down from Upstate New York to help us. She accepted our offer on a Thursday and drove down that Monday, ready for work. The journey had begun; it is through this journey that most of my practical knowledge formed.

During this book, I'll touch on the lessons I learned while growing from a three-man company to one with over one hundred employees that had been featured on the Inc. 5000 list of fastest-growing American companies for two consecutive years. These lessons helped me understand just how tough it can be for the little guy trying to run a shop and make a living. In this book, I'll relay those challenges and experiences, breaking it back down to explain why I think smaller operations are the best way for the mortgage brokerage industry to resurrect itself and move forward, due largely to the onslaught of regulations we now face. This book will also help consumers get an insider's look at what's going on in the industry, and how it affects them—none of it is pretty, and none of it is to the consumer's benefit as far as I can tell. These changes lead to more costs being paid by the consumer and a prolonged, time-consuming process because of all the third parties that are now involved and taking a cut of the money.

So let's get started!

First, I'll go over the changes that occurred from roughly 2009 to 2012, discuss the reality of the factors changed by the Dodd–Frank reform, and then I'll segue into a more positive planning and growth section. I will follow this up with a section depicting successful and not-so-successful practices and will then bring us up to the most recent changes in late 2015, particularly the inception of the TILA-RESPA Integrated Disclosure (TRID) rule.

Currently, I am both a mortgage broker and a banker with my own warehouse line. I employ six loan officers and have a staff of four assistants. I am licensed in ten states and am currently active in five of those as we downsize in preparation for increased rates and the slowing refinance market. My shop is on track to do between $50 million and $60 million in loan volume with a revenue of between $1.5 and $1.7 million. By comparison, in 2013, Ikon did $367 million in loan volume with revenues right at $12.5 million, but that was accomplished with over six-ty loan officers. The main issues were that while achiev-ing this level of volume, we have faced ever-changing, strict regulations that have led to fines and even consent orders in two states.

We'll discuss regulations in depth in other chapters, but the bottom line is that in this case, working on a smaller scale has proven to be move viable and profitable. I think the smaller-shop model is the key to survival when deal-ing with regulation changes in our industry. However, I think it would be next to impossible for a one-man shop to stay operating in the long term. At a minimum, the one-man shop needs strategic partnerships and a pleth-ora of tools in their toolbox. After the 2008 meltdown, I was one of the many who thought we needed some change, but I think they went a little too far with some of the corrections they made. However, I also see some light on the horizon, representing a possible change for the better. As mentioned, later in the book, we'll discuss the changes with TRID that went into effect in October of 2015, and you'll discover that I believe some of the items within this regulation are better for both consumers and mortgage brokers. In particular, they seem to be a little easier for the consumer to understand.

My plan is to create a series of reference texts for the smaller mortgage broker, whether you operate a one-man shop or are part of a small- to mid-sized operation similar to ours. Hopefully this book and those that follow it will prove to be invaluable tools placed in your mortgage broker's toolbox.

2

Industry Overview

AFTER THE MELTDOWN in 2008, we saw a lot of indus-tries in flux. The big banks got their bailouts and looked for someone to blame for creating such back-ward, risk-filled products instead of themselves, so they pointed their fingers at the mortgage broker. "It has to be the small mortgage broker; they sent all the crappy paper." In some cases that may be true, but let's ask a few simple questions: Did mortgage brokers create state income products? Did they create the option ARM or the infamous <u>mortgage derivative</u>? Did they develop the subprime market with lower lending stan-dards? The answer is no. The mortgage broker, by definition, offers product options—and these were the products they were given to sell.

The banks had wholesale departments, and the basic concept was simple: "Hey, we can have mortgage brokers handle the mortgages to consumers and offer them lower, 'wholesale' rates. We will, in turn, underwrite these files and end up with only the profitable mortgages, leaving out the needless and expensive things like branches the banks really don't want anyway. Just about any banker will tell you he or she would prefer everything being electronic—not have tellers and never have to see clients—as a basic business model. In today's world of fees and costs, they are literally encouraging you not to set foot in their branch.

Just the other day, I noticed a fee for depositing cash. Yep, they would rather get your money and never have to actually deal with you, the customer. With banks getting out of the wholesale front line, they've turned their attention to their retail operations. In most cases, they positioned themselves behind some of the newer mid-level banks, giving them large lines of credit so that when the mid-level banks eventually have mortgage buybacks, they'll have a deeper pocket from which to pick.

For those uncertain of what a mortgage buyback is: to put it simply, it is when there is either an issue with the paper to the investor via the underwriter or a default occurs within a stated period of time. For example, if the borrower defaults in the first twelve months, the originator of that loan—the investor bank—is on the hook to repurchase or "buy back" the paper. Another form of a buyback is if there was an issue with the underwriting of the loan. Brokers often don't see the buyback hit them directly, and as a mini-<u>correspondent</u>, the broker acts as a banker, with limited risk. Big banks like Wells Fargo and Bank of America were taught a harsh lesson by the amount of paper they got stuck with due to buybacks from Fannie Mae and Freddie Mac. This led them to move out of wholesale and only take positions with retail, as more of a "super correspondent" position behind the much larger group of new mid-tier investors.

What does this mean for the local mortgage broker? Simply put, the big banks are returning to a conservative model with higher credit scores and fewer products. This presents opportunities for the local mortgage broker through niche products and access to investors who are willing to lend to those with lower credit scores. We have seen many referrals come our way due to our niche products, as well as referrals for borrowers whose scores fall below the 640 mid-score line. There are lenders out there that will offer government-backed loans to applicants with as low as a 550 credit score, and this presents another opportunity to both local mortgage brokers and correspondent lenders.

The relationship between mortgage brokers and the big banks wasn't very different: They want us to lend their money, but they also want to blame us if something goes wrong. The single biggest point to remember is, if you were brokering the loan, ultimately the bank was underwriting the file, issuing the products available, setting the rates, and deciding whether or not to ultimately do the deal.

After Fannie and Freddie nearly went under and their "approval" became more of a maybe than a solid-gold promise, we started to see the consolidation of the industry. One by one, those big banks involved in wholesale went under or ceased operations in that particular branch of the industry. Without getting too bogged down in names, the main players during 2009–2012 included big banks like Wells Fargo, Bank of America, Chase, Fifth Third, and CitiMortgage all got out of wholesale. They were replaced largely with mid-level lenders that almost nobody had heard of: lenders including Flagstar, Stonegate Mortgage, Stearns, and Franklin American.

This consolidation led to a larger consolidation in the industry, with lenders more often opting for mini-correspondent or full-correspondent lending. That might not mean much to the general public; this is when a broker steps up a level and now has a large line of credit that allows them to fund their own loans. A mini-correspondent would still have the investor underwrite the deal, while a full-correspondent would underwrite his or her own deals. The largest growth within our industry has been the expansion of full-correspondent channels like Quicken, Guaranteed Rate, Benchmark Mortgage, and numerous others who grew and in the process consolidated loan officers into their channels. In most cases, they issue their own rates and use a secondary pricing plan to fund their own loans; then they sell directly to larger investors like SunTrust, Wells Fargo, Chase, etc. Most of this growth can be attributed to the 2010 <u>Dodd-Frank Wall Street Reform and Consumer Protection Act</u>, which changed the industry as a whole by limiting and in most cases reducing lender compensation models. This act essentially brought the mortgage industry to a model much more in line with what you'd see in real estate, for Realtors. We'll dive into more of the practical effects of Dodd-Frank in later chapters, but for now, know that it was a catalyst for consolidation.

Dodd-Frank led to the outlawing of the <u>yield spread premium (YSP)</u> and, to most brokers, are no longer able to receive payment on the front and the back ends. Looking back at it, five years later, I see it did raise the bar, as it meant that to go from broker to the next level, a person would have to take on more risk and responsibility for the loans he or she issued. It also created more transparency; the consumer could no longer hide fees being earned on the back end via YSP. The days of one on the front and two on the back were gone, never to be seen again. Again, this wasn't a bad thing, as it got rid of a lot of the low-end guys that couldn't sell a rate and couldn't explain how they earned their money.

Dodd-Frank occurred on the heels of the Secure and Fair Enforcement (SAFE) Mortgage Licensing Act of 2008; with these acts combined, the most significant changes in the mortgage industry in the last few decades occurred. The most important facets of both acts created a larger threshold and an increased education requirement for licensees. Someone starting in our industry now faces a standard similar to what I saw at Merrill Lynch in 2002. They cannot speak to clients or quote rates until all of their licensing is done. The testing is much harder, and there's also a patchwork of state licensing to deal with. While passing the National SAFE Act test is a major hurdle, the timelines upheld by some individual states is cause for serious delay. We have seen some states take as long as six months to approve an individual. Some states, like New York, will not approve new companies, period. On average, it will take two to three months for a state to approve a new company license. This has led to a lot of frustration and confusion in our industry.

Initially, it was here that we created our niche with Ikon Financial Group; we began to consolidate loan officers and grow the company. The plan was to attract loan officers in this time of flux.

3

Moving Forward

W ITH THE ADVENT of the National Mortgage Licensing System (NMLS) and the higher education requirement for brokers, it is more important than ever to plan ahead for success. One of the largest issues we ran into when trying to grow was the constantly changing regulations and the patchwork of differences in those regulations across the nation. This led me to realize that in our industry, smaller may actually be better.

We ran into a number of issues with individual loan officers in other markets who seemed unable to follow and/or know the rules. In some cases, I'll take the responsibility for not providing proper education, but the issue was more logistics than anything else. At one point, we had branches in eleven states, from Maryland to Florida, all the way over to Texas and back up to Idaho. This model of operating multiple branches didn't work for us and I seriously doubt it would work for anyone who wasn't a full-correspondent.

If you plan on becoming a broker or lender, I believe that staying smaller will be better than building a large enterprise. The main reason is that all the responsibility falls on ownership any way you cut it, so you must have complete control over every loan offered by your shop. Even with centralized processing, it was a logistical nightmare given the changes that constantly came down the pipe. Add to that the new layer of ObamaCare, and for me, the writing was on the wall. It was time to downsize; the decision was made to sell the majority of Ikon's assets and branches and consolidate to a few locations in our home market of Charleston, South Carolina.

The introduction of NMLS brought a number of changes in our industry's licensing processes, and I think they will be for the better in the long run. Now all members of our industry are held accountable and their information is recorded across multiple jobs, including any infractions. That being said, I think there are some obvious issues with the system as it is currently set up, and there is little consistency across the states in terms of audits and fines. I also feel that some states look for any reason to fine a brokerage shop as part of a standard practice. Take the following as a case in point: We had applied for and received a license in the state of California. We did not end up opening a branch or performing any transactions in California. We received a notice that we would be audited, with which we fully complied. I was then sent a bill for $5,000 to cover the cost of the audit. Keep in mind that we had closed no transactions and, therefore, had no information for them to review in terms of business done in California; yet they felt it necessary to charge us $5,000 for the pleasure of not doing business within their state.

Compare that to more user-friendly states like Virginia or Tennessee, where audits have been handled both in person and electronically with no issues— and nothing in terms of cost like our neighbor to the far west. I would like to see the NMLS do something to make business operation costs consistent across the nation, but I know that's probably unrealistic.

Let's touch briefly on consent orders and their impact on the industry. Anyone who looks up my name or my company will see that we accepted a couple of consent orders. This is the very reason I'm convinced that smaller will be better. Both cases dealt with issues we had in branches outside of South Carolina that weren't covered properly, which led to ownership, myself, taking responsibility for others' actions. I do not fault the states for doing their jobs, but I do think, given the nature of our business, it's that much more important to maintain control over every single file attached to your license. Going forward, you need to be able to take advantage of the licensing changes that allow you to do business in multiple states; therefore, it's incredibly important to act responsibly with regards to you and your company's licensing.

After the experiences mentioned above, I would strongly suggest that if you ever face an issue with the regulatory body in a market outside your own, you hire an attorney to deal with the problem. Make sure that you have the phone number of an attorney capable of representing you in any state in which you plan to do business. Unfortunately, as the level of regulations grows, you will need experienced attorneys should something come up that could affect your license. From my own experiences, as long as you handle the matter properly, a consent order is not a death sentence in our industry. If you take the approach of sticking your head in the sand, it will come back to haunt you later.

That being said, in our situations, I think the regulators were fair. We've moved on from both issues and are still doing business in other states. In both cases, the solution was to agree to no longer operate in those specific states. In my case, this worked out, as I didn't have licenses in those states prior to the issues, and I didn't do business in them either. The lesson learned? Owners have to take responsibility for the actions of all the individuals under them.

The multi-state license is the only thing that makes walking this tightrope with various states worthwhile. For Internet marketing to work for refinances, you must work from a subsection of populated areas. If you live in a smaller state like I do, it becomes all the more important to be able to expand past the borders. In my opinion, continuing to operate as a mortgage broker is made possible by the ability to become licensed in other states; this is due to the pricing advantage we hold over most, if not all, banks. Having the ability to advertise a price on Bankrate or LendingTree is a great equalizer for smaller shops, especially if your systems are dialed in to allow you to close many conventional deals.

Another strategy I used was to keep a warehouse line open for conventional business. There is some added expense with related fees, third-party document preparation, and interest costs, but I have found it to be invaluable in terms of doing business. We're able to have a significant pricing advantage over any bank, and we're able to control the issuing of our funds. Are there some factors I'd like to have more control over? Sure, but at the same time, I think it's just the right ratio of risk to reward to make it worthwhile. My approach is to also broker some deals—namely our <u>Federal Housing Association (FHA)</u> and some smaller, more conventional loan sizes—where using the warehouse line would not be cost efficient. There are higher capital requirements for using these lines, but the money you make as a result of having them certainly makes it attractive.

In hindsight, after my experiences as a mortgage professional trying to grow quickly in our industry, going the route of a small, high-quality shop with fewer employees and less overhead is the best path to success. I have a hard time believing that loan officers at banks will be able to work for peanuts for a long period of time, but that's the model the banks want to establish. As time goes on and the regulations become more a part of the system, I think we'll see a number of bankers return to the broker model. I, for one, plan to be here, and through sharing my experiences, hopefully I can help a few brokers be there with me.

4

How to Succeed as a Mortgage Broker

T IME FOR US to move in a more positive and productive direction. Like a shark, you need to always move forward to stay alive, and hopefully sections like this one will prove value to both mortgage brokers and those trying to understand how to sell mortgages.

I will deliver this part in outline format and leave some sections open-ended for future improvement. I am reminded of a saying from my first employer in this industry: "*Kaizen*," which in Japan is a philosophy focused on practicing for continuous improvement in all aspects of life and business—or, said more simply, "Improve yourself every day."

1. Organize and Time Block

I see these as the most important aspects of becoming a highly successful loan officer. Too often I encounter loan officers who allow their pipelines to control them, which will eventually limit their production levels because they fail to continue prospecting at all times. I've broken it down as the "Three Ps": Prep, Prospecting, and Production—always in that order. You can start with any one of the three, but you must proceed in the aforementioned sequence.

The time spent preparing, prospecting, and in production is time spent well, as this is what mortgage professionals are expected and required to do for their company. I've set up our marketing systems and processing to help my loan officers achieve the highest possible efficiency. There are only so many workable hours in a day; time is a commodity you cannot recover or recreate. Given all the hurdles we now have in place with TRID and up-front disclosures, it is important to meet deadlines and recapture referral business every day.

By using time blocking and planning in advance, you can help yourself and your people maximize productivity each day. Obviously, the following examples are for individuals who have completed their licensing. That being said, I do usually have employees who are still going through the licensing process come in to the office every day so they can listen to and learn from those around them.

YEAR ONE

The following is an example of a time-blocking schedule best for fresher loan officers. In year one, I typically have all junior loan officers report directly to me or to a senior loan officer so the placement, disclosure, and pricing of their deals can be reviewed.

A typical workweek would be as follows:

Monday–Thursday:

8:30–9:00	Arrive and prep.
9:00–12:00	Train, meet with senior loan officers, prepare rates for the day, follow-up on the previous day's work, prospect pipeline management, and work dedicated websites.
12:00–1:00	Designated lunch period.
1:00–7:00	Prospecting: spending call time on the phone with prospects.

Friday:

9:00–11:00 or 12:00 Review the workweek with senior management, go over game plan for the following week.

Our geographic market is one that typically winds down early on Fridays. With our warmer weather, we see that clients and supporting third parties often take advantage of a shorter workweek and shut down early on Fridays to head to the beach. Depending on your market, you can choose to extend the workweek and get more hours in. I am always quite successful calling prospects on Saturdays—in fact, I find we get a higher success ratio on reaching the clients during the weekend—and I would prefer to call around on a Saturday versus a Friday afternoon. I always like to work files already in progress to the end of the day on Fridays and prep for the following week. Additionally, we sometimes go on-site with our building partners during the weekends; it's a good idea to let the loan officers off early on Friday if they're working Saturday or Sunday.

Think of your schedule as being in two blocks. The first block, from 9:00–12:00 is **PREP**. The second period, from 1:00–7:00, is **PROSPECT**. The mornings are used for follow-up, for determining who to call that day, and for training. We have set items for junior officers to learn about during this time. Training is done in various groups and includes software, products, marketing, calling, sales, and lender-specific training led by lender representatives. During the morning, newer loan officers should set up Internet leads to call and work on viral marketing, blogging, following up with leads, and database management. Preparing to make calls is key for a new loan officer to be successful early in his or her career. If you, the owner of the company, don't give them a road map to success, it's likely they'll go off course from time to time.

By keeping the schedule simple and consistent, you will help new loan officers gain a greater knowledge of your products and the processes by which you attract business in exterior markets. Please note that at no time are you expected to leave the office for prospecting purposes. We tend to keep all junior loan officers in the office working on some type of Internet leads, whether they be purchase leads or refinance leads. I do this mainly because they're not ready to act as a representative of your company to the general public.

YEAR TWO

The first year concentrates on how to get business in the door. Without this building block, there really is no reason to spend significant time on the second phase of their education. As loan officers complete year one, their responsibilities as a mortgage professional will begin to increase.

The focus of the second year is how to place, produce, and close a loan. A different set of skills are needed to fully grasp how loans progress through lenders' systems. The second year works with the Three Ps. In year one, junior officers were introduced to the first two Ps: PREP and PROSPECT.

During the first year, a senior loan officer or the company owner handles everything for newer loan officers, from issuing and organizing necessary paperwork to processing it. In year two, more of these responsibilities go to the loan officers.

With this in mind, we'll vary the time blocks some, and we'll add the third and arguably the most important P: PRODUCTION. Simply put, production is the processing of a file through an underwriting system to result in a closing and, thus, $$$$$.

We incorporate the third P by breaking up the six-hour block previously used for prospecting and including a three-hour period for production.

We'll keep the same workweek we had in the first year, but feel free to vary how you do things. This type of schedule is also where I would start if there were more senior loan officers who wanted to take their production to the next level. Following is an example of a year-two schedule:

Monday:

9:00–12:00	Prep.
12:00–1:00	Lunch.
1:00–4:00	Prospect.
4:00–7:00	Production.

Let's say you have a large pipeline of loans in that week. Your Tuesday might look like this:

9:00–12:00	Production.
12:00–1:00	Lunch.
1:00–4:00	Prep.
4:00–7:00	Prospect.

The reason Tuesday is structured this way is so the loan officer can focus on his or her loans in the morning so those items can be completed that day. Think of the flow of work. If you submit items to the underwriter in the morning, they will be closer to the front of the line for review. We also now have a prospecting period at the end of the business day, which is typically a good time to reach borrowers as they are winding down their own day at the office.

The next question you might ask is: Why do I work on all of these each day, and why in this order? The answer is simple: You will not accomplish as much if you get stuck on just production. You may prospect very hard for some time, get tired of it, and decide to focus only on producing loans. At this point, you'll reach a level of maximum capacity. We are trying to keep loan officers from falling into this rut. Each officer's capacity is different; a poor habit we want to avoid is when a loan officer gets, say, five loans in the pipeline and focuses completely on following those five loans through the process to closing. This is *not the method* we teach.

Instead, I teach loan officers that in order to be successful, they must work on each of the Three Ps, in order, each day. The reason for doing so in this specific order is simple. You need to prep to determine which prospects are ready to be called. You will be more efficient if you have a game plan for that day (i.e., a list of names to call and for what purpose). New leads will come in during your prospecting period and go to the top of your to-call list. After you prep, you follow through on the plan by prospecting. By having a plan in place, you can again increase your efficiency by only calling prospects you've either emailed during your prep period or with whom you've previously set up a follow-up plan. Again, efficiency is the key. The final item each day is production. Always be aware of where loans are in the process. Are you missing an item you can get? Does your processor need help reaching out to a client? During year one, this is all going on behind the scenes to close your loans. In year two, we add these tasks to your list.

The thought process behind the distinction between these years is simple. During year one, you are learning the ins and outs and figuring out how to approach prospects; this is why you will spend the majority of your day refining this skill. By year two, you should have improved to a level that allows for increased efficiency. In effect, you should be able to close a higher percentage of prospects in your second year because you know what to say and, more importantly, *how to say it*.

For each time block, there are specific tasks to be performed.

Prep or Planning

This time is reserved for organizing and preparing to make sales calls. To make effective sales calls, you should set up time to contact prospects via email and to set expectations for your calls. This time block is best used emailing clients, researching, setting up call lists, organizing, and preparing. As Louis Pasteur said, "Chance favors the prepared mind." The leads that are provided to you will often require work in the form of information-gathering. Identify those leads who need to be contacted either by when they entered your system or if it is a purchase lead or direct referral.

Work items for this period:

- Email rate quotes to prospects.
- Update welcome notices from purchase websites.
- Update your Realtor partners on purchase websites.
- Email informational articles to prospects.
- Work through valid refinance leads for dedicated call time.
- Prepare scripts for product-specific calls.
- Prepare with a senior loan officer for follow-up calls.
- Build your own call lists.
- Design fliers for Realtor partners.

- Email follow-ups to Internet leads.
- Email follow-ups to referrals.

Prospecting

This is a period for making phone calls to prospects. No other work should be done at this time. Just make prospecting phone calls and follow up with email prospects and previously contacted clients. During this time, you don't make personal calls; you don't even leave the room. This is your time for making money and taking applications. Applications will happen at any given time, but this is a dedicated period for focused effort.

If you have junior loan officers or team members working under you, as the owner of the company, it is important to listen to what is being said and to make sure they have scripts prepared for each type of call. If you're making your own calls, the most important aspect of this time block is to avoid interruptions that are not related to prospecting for new business.

Production

This time block will require you to be present with your processors. If you are a single-man operation, you will need to dedicate this time solely to production-related items. To do a significant amount of volume, you will need processors and assistants helping you, especially with the number of new disclosures and laws changing like quicksand under your feet. The key to doing a lot of production is being able to delegate responsibility to other team members, whether it be following up on conditions or calling new prospects.

The most important aspect of time blocking is that you fit each activity into your day.

As the need for constant prospecting has grown, so has the need for compliance. A loan officer who doesn't pay attention to compliance and those aspects of the job that require it is setting him or herself up for future failure. Being compliant means making sure the necessary items are in line for disclosure, timelines are set, and preparation for new items with TRID has been completed in accordance with the regulations set by your state. Now that we have discussed how to properly manage your time throughout your day, let's move on to utilizing the tools that are available.

2. Database Management

The most significant tool in an experienced loan officer's toolbox is his or her database and its contents.

I currently use several databases for different aspects of managing clients and referral sources. Some have better features for completing a particular task than others. I have tried out systems like those held in Point, Encompass, Mortgage Matters, Vantage Production, and LeadMailbox. Each has pluses and minuses; what is most important is that you use *some* type of system for automated responses, data organization, and marketing for top-of-mind awareness.

Overall, our marketing plan includes strong database management, niche-specific marketing, ironclad purchase business alliances with BoomTown and Vantage Production, the ability to refinance loans through LowerMyBills.com (which provides a way for you to market across multiple states) or another source, and consistent Realtor marketing.

BoomTown is a unique purchase lead system superior to other lead generation sites I've tried. It will primarily be used for purchases in your local market, if available. There are a number of other sites providing similar services; as you evaluate these companies, remember that the most important aspect is the partnership you have in place with the Realtor from that company with whom you work. We have tried using BoomTown in external markets with less success, as we weren't able to build that one-on-one relationship with the Realtor team with whom we worked. BoomTown provides search engine optimization (SEO) for your Realtor's website, helping to drive traffic through search engines like Google, Yahoo, and Bing. If you plan to work with an SEO generation system, make sure it's in compliance, delivering the lead to you and the agent at the same time. It is also important that the Realtor be tech-savvy and fully engaged in the process. We've experienced the good and the bad, having worked both with responsive Realtors and with those who don't see the lead's value.

BoomTown has a database management system that's geared toward Realtors, but it offers the ability to export leads to other database systems that are more geared toward mortgage professionals. While you have the ability to email and otherwise export information from the database, it's not set up to be used for any type of <u>drip campaign</u> or mortgage-specific marketing.

Vantage Production and Mortgage Matters are similar systems that can both tie into your operating system, allowing it to use the data in a mortgage-focused marketing software. I prefer Vantage's system over Mortgage Matters's for two reasons: cost and the quality of the marketing material. Vantage's system has more options and is constantly updated with new materials on almost a weekly basis. Mortgage Matters required a little more legwork in terms of branding items and costs almost four times more than Vantage to initially set up. Both have monthly fees based upon usage. I brand all company materials to reflect the owner instead of the individual loan officers. The reason is rather obvious: We are currently seeing high turnover in our industry, so it's wise to protect your data and past clients. Vantage and Mortgage Matters are mortgage-specific platforms for managing past clients. Point and Encompass have some marketing features, but they aren't, in my opinion, as high quality as what you see with Vantage or Mortgage Matters.

Also, I try to vary my Internet leads by prospecting a mixture of purchases and refinances. Currently, in 2015, we are experiencing lower refinance interest rates. A significant portion of the market has been hit hard in recent years, and this is why I've been focusing on LowerMyBills.com—they have a mixture of products, including debt consolidation. When rates go back up, this will create another interest cycle, and having a connection with a refinancing firm can ensure that you have options for the next rate-dip in the cycle.

With a combination of purchasing new leads and marketing to existing and previous clients, a good broker should be able to generate multiple deals each month.

3. Targeting Realtors

Our second phase of marketing involves targeting the top hundred to two hundred Realtors in the local market. The 80/20 rule applies here: 20 percent of a sales force generates 80 percent of the business. Using this principle, we'll only focus sales efforts on the top 20 percent of Realtors in your area. Why would you want to spend time and effort on Realtors who don't close deals? Do not waste time on unproductive Realtors. Use realty sales data to review Realtor contacts. Strive to focus your efforts on the top 20 percent of the market in your branches' locations.

4. Niche-Specific Marketing

Next, we'll focus on niche-specific marketing. Examples include U.S. Department of Veteran Affairs (VA), FHA, debt consolidation, and builder marketing. We have simple strategies for reaching a specific, niche market to grow your business. Part of our philosophy is to spread out the net and diversify where you market and how you go about growing your mortgage business. Our VA campaigns include using particular lists from ListSource, which we contact through a large letter campaign followed by postcards on a monthly basis through either our internal system or In Touch Today.

Many niche-specific campaigns can utilize List-Source. We recommend them because they are owned by First American Title Insurance Company, and the records they keep for mailing campaigns are accurate and complete. We have spent many hours researching in order to provide our branches with access to the best possible list-building company.

In Touch Today is a quality database mailing company that has competitive pricing for postcard and letter campaigns. We use it for a weekly email blast containing mortgage facts for your Realtor clients. We wouldn't recommend using In Touch Today for individual clients, as our customer management system handles all client contacts for you via Vantage. Niche specific marketing is extremely effective when properly used. This should be something you and your team practice monthly.

5. Mass or Target Mailings

Mass or target mailing is another avenue we use with positive results. Our system involves dropping blocks of five thousand envelopes at a time. This generally results in about eight deals after answering roughly fifty to seventy-five calls coming in to the 800 number listed on the mailer. We have better results when we target areas that are closer to our location. We vary the product advertised on the mailers we send out; we'll focus on <u>FHA streamlines</u>, <u>VA Interest Rate Reduction Refinance Loans (IRRRLs)</u>, FHA converting to conventional loans, and Home Affordable Refinance Program (HARP) loans. While I personally haven't closed many HARP loans, we consistently have success with FHA streamline loans and FHA conversions.

The mailing service we use is Camber Marketing based out of Atlanta, Georgia. The standout features for me, as the owner of the company, is that the database is given to us in full and the email tracking, which allows me to see each call as it comes in—and which loan officer got the call. Other available data includes caller ID when available and call duration so you know if the loan officer actually answered the call. Once the name goes into our operating system, Vantage instantly stores the data in your back-office marketing system. When you're able to track who is calling, who is answering, and how long the call lasted, you're able to gain a lot of valuable insight as to who your exact target market and client is.

6. Multi-State Marketing

Licensing is the key to making this system work, and one of the game-changers for a mortgage broker is to become licensed in multiple states. I see this as the most important, beneficial change that has occurred in the last five years, as it allows a broker to reach multiple marketplaces—with the right marketing plan. I have found that marketing in other states works best for refinances. It seems to me that Realtors, clients, and loan officers are best served by sticking to local transactions for their purchase business. Clients enjoy and trust the local aspect of it. They are usually unfamiliar with the home buying process and have peace of mind knowing you're only a few miles down the road and not a voice over the phone. You can still use Internet lead systems like BoomTown and TigerLeads to create multi-state campaigns with your marketing partners. However, my suggestion is to focus out-of-state business on only refinances.

7. Niche Products

Niche products are making a comeback, which opens the doors for brokers to find success by taking advantage of these additional options. When I began in the industry, there was a saying: "Mortgage brokers present options." Going forward, that is exactly what brokers should keep presenting to the general public. Banks aren't going to lend with niche products at this point; as brokers, we should take advantage of this opportunity. These niche products include bank statement programs, past negative real estate events such as a bankruptcy, foreclosure, or short sale, and loans operating on investor cash flow only. These products need to become tools in your arsenal, helping you to get more deals.

Given the changes that have occurred since the 2008 meltdown, in most cases, investors offering niche products have to keep them on their books—or with a partially owned subsidiary. This means that if you lend money on a niche product, you must stay with it, for better or for worse. Because it forces investors and banks to stand by their products, I think it's one of the more responsible acts taken by Congress. Anyone familiar with the issues created by mortgage-backed securitization when investors got left holding the bag will agree with me that this is a positive change.

Will it ultimately be different this time around? I think so, as the investors releasing niche products have accountability, and I also think these loans will help mortgage brokers in presenting options to those people affected by the 2008 meltdown. Then the loan officer can later refinance them to more traditional loans as their overall credit profile improves and the "mortgage events" drift further and further into the past.

8. Working with Home Builders

As the economy picks back up, so does the home-building industry. Our market has seen continuous job growth, with some major industry leaders like Boeing and Volvo taking root in our arena. This, among other factors, helped the home-building industry survive, and as of 2014, it has grown to a solid level with some national builders in operation and regional builders taking the lead. For the smaller mortgage broker or a shop of our size (six loan officers), it's best to focus on the regional and local builders.

One advantage the compensation changes have given us is the ability to offer lender credits based on the overage of the compensation model a broker chooses. These funds are available on all FHA loans since we broker these transactions, and our pricing advantage on conventional loans allows us to also offer lender credits to the consumer. I have my team focus on offering better service and spending time on-site with our local builders. This option may not be available to a one-man shop due to the fact you're spending all of your time in one location. In order to still achieve that relationship with a builder, in lieu of spending time, you will have to spend money to help with promotional campaigns and open houses they are holding.

When promoting products that involve our builder partners, we offer a rate match guarantee along with seller and lender credits. We match what our builders offer, which is pretty much the standard in our market and what I assume is the standard across the nation. Some larger mortgage shops enter into marketing agreements with national builders, but I think that will lead to more issues and potential regulation fines for both parties. Some national builders in our market are going back to the simple method of referring three lenders and having all three of those lenders offer the same lender credit. I believe this is the route most builders will take as the market picks up. Builders should be building homes, not worrying about the mortgage side of the equation. That is the key for maintaining a successful relationship with a builder: to communicate and provide clients responsive service and solutions to their problems.

9. Advertising

Promotion can be simple and should be effective. Given the changes in laws that have occurred and may occur in the future, you must ensure all advertising materials are in compliance with state regulations. We have seen success by marketing niche products with an overview, meaning we don't state interest rates and instead focus on the availability of the product to a target audience that believes they cannot currently purchase a home. Most of the promotional items we currently use are incredibly simple information pieces directed to Realtors. You can use a local printing shop, and keep in mind that most of the investors will have flyers already created for their products—so in a lot of cases, you don't have to worry about designing the ad.

Currently, we primarily advertise the newer niche products since everyone has similar conventional products rates. We are also going old-school by using basic signage on-site with our builders. The signs we use on site simply state who we are and how to reach us. Don't confuse the person driving or walking by. When you're able to advertise effectively without breaking the bank, you're going to remain in business.

10. Social Media

Social media is the wave of the future; if you don't understand or mesh with it, to properly integrate it into your business, you either need to hire someone who understands it or outsource to a company that can handle it for you. I've tried both methods; going the route of hiring a social-media-minded employee is far more cost effective than paying a social media marketing business.

We've dedicated an entire chapter of this book to social media, and it was written with the input and help of one of my employees. It is *that* important; I don't want to tell you to go to Foursquare when I really mean LinkedIn or even Spotify. You get my point: If you don't know how to do something, hire someone who does.

11. Internet Marketing

Online marketing has become essential in today's business world. The next time you're driving down the road, look into the cars around you and see where not only the passengers' eyes are focused, but where the drivers' eyes are, too. Are they looking up at the billboards towering above the road? Are they checking out the signs planted in yards and medians at stoplights? No, they're looking down at their phone!

If you haven't already, you need to create and establish an online presence. A lot of people have the misconception that Internet marketing is expensive. It absolutely does not have to be. We will dive into this deeper later in this book.

12. Website

One piece we haven't touched on yet is your website. We use ours as an informative front door and to give customers peace of mind that they're working with a legitimate operation. Make sure your website is compliant with your state's laws, as different states require information referencing licensing in their part of the country to be displayed on the site. Any state in which you have an active license will have rules and regulations governing your website.

We don't focus on SEO to increase our web presence. Instead of spending money in that area, to drive traffic to our site, we purchase actual Internet leads. Depending on your budget, this may be an option. We focus our dollars on a hands-on approach with boots on the ground. I would rather have my guys at lunch with a Realtor or spreading information pieces to the public than spending money to drive people who might not even be interested in buying a home to our website.

We do have an online application link, but given the level of disclosure and amount of information needed to complete the application, I require my loan officers to call online applicants to check for accuracy. Roughly 85 percent of online applications filled out by the consumer are missing information that would slow down the process—and you'll end up having to call them anyway. So use this as an opportunity to personally interact with the client and potentially sell more.

13. Diversify Income Streams

Recently, we've begun to diversify the streams of income that are coming into the brokerage company.

I invested in commercial real estate and lost. I've been purchasing property to use as rental homes since 2005, so I've seen the good and the bad. I think it's a natural fit for a mortgage broker to own rental property because as an expert in the industry, you know what's out there and will recognize a good deal when you see one. I find buying foreclosed homes with cash and fixing them up fun, and it's something I'm sure I will keep doing. A few years ago, I started doing this within the company; we currently own several properties that allow for some revenue to come into the company that isn't dependent on closing loans.

There are other avenues available to a mortgage broker. One such revenue stream is selling biweekly payment plans via escrow-licensed companies. We use GemCap, a company based in Chicago; they are more than willing to sign up individual loan officers or a company. There is a fee for their service; you earn a commission based on the payment that's escrowed. For example, if the payment is $1,000, we would typically charge $500 to set up the service. It is very simple to set up and, in most cases, helps cut years off the clients' mortgages. These numbers add up, and we find that roughly 20 to 30 percent of our clients are interested in this type of product.

Another revenue option that requires much more legwork and proper disclosure is to get licensed to sell mortgage protection insurance. Check with your state to find out what disclosures are required. Anyone carrying both licenses will need to get registered, take the coursework, and fully disclose to clients that they will earn a commission on both sales. Which, if you think about it, is the way it should be. A typical mortgage protection policy will pay the entire first year's premium as commission. Mortgage protection is a term life product, so it's a one-time sale, but each one would pay a commission of between $400 and $1,000 depending on the insurance agency through whom you hold your license.

Mailer companies that offer names and addresses of mortgage holders to their clients (other insurance agents) won't actually get this data until the mortgages are formally recorded. In most markets, this means about forty-five to sixty days after the deal is closed. This is another advantage the mortgage broker has: In this equation, you've already made direct contact with the client, and you know when the mortgage closes. For a one-man shop, this could mean big bucks if you can offer both a biweekly payment plan and a mortgage protection plan.

A few words of caution: Biweekly plans don't pay out quickly, as most companies first require that the borrower get the full payment in place. We've found the best time to sell the biweekly is directly after the closing, as the borrower won't have a mortgage payment to make that month since the loan is either resetting for a refinance or is new. This is another good add-on to make the loans you sell even more profitable.

Most mortgage protection insurance companies will have a one-year recapture period. This means if your client cancels the policy within the first year, you may have to return the commission. Before signing up with an agency, educate yourself and ask about their policy and think of how it could affect you.

The ideal situation is one in which the term policy is paid completely upfront. That's not realistic for each client, but remember: We're looking to diversify your revenue. If you were strictly a life insurance agent, you probably wouldn't be reading this book.

A seasoned loan officer may consider getting a property and casualty license so he or she can write property insurance. This is a little difficult because of steering rules. Where a mortgage protection policy is a post-closing product, homeowners insurance is necessary for the transaction to occur. Various states have different rules in reference to whether you can even have and use this type of license. If you're a single producer, I suggest exploring your options and checking with the regulatory bodies for both mortgages and insurance in your home state.

One side note: Some groups have been offering to pay loan officers for credit repair services. In our state of South Carolina, it is not legal to act as both a mortgage broker and a credit counseling officer. Check with your state to see if it's legal or not. The potential commissions from credit repair are nothing in comparison to what you bring in as a mortgage broker. We typically refer individuals to other companies that offer these types of services, with no commission expectation.

Another way to increase revenue is to offer credit reporting services. Our services give potential score-boosters for our clients, and most of our investors allow for rescores either during the process or prior to submission. The ability to give someone information to improve their scores can help you salvage deals. Ultimately, it is always up to the borrower; if they want to purchase a home or refinance, they need to take care of their credit profile.

We've discussed time management, utilizing your database(s), how to use mailers, strengthening your relationships with relators and builders, and creating multiples streams of income. It is now time to dive deep into using social media platforms in the most effective and efficient ways possible.

5

Being Effective on Social Media

IF YOU TRULY want to be successful as a mortgage broker, you have to make yourself available and known across a variety of platforms. Twenty years ago, and even just ten years ago, this wasn't an issue. You could simply send letters, call some prospects, and make a heck of a living.

The attention of our audience has shifted. Throughout this chapter, we'll discuss social media selling, how to build a strong foundation, and provide a simple guide to creating and utilizing social platforms as efficiently as possible.

Selling is not the same as it used to be. Remember when we lived in a world—*not that long ago*—where we'd get excited when the home phone rang or the doorbell sounded, and we'd happily answer? We would be thrilled to receive a piece of mail, whether it was a letter from grandma or a sporting goods store's monthly catalog. We lived in a world where after spending eight minutes waiting for dial-up to get on the Internet, we'd open every email—no matter what! This *was* human interaction.

Between 2006 and 2009, we lived in a world where Facebook and Twitter seemed uninterrupted; we could log in at any time to find out what our friends were doing or to catch up with them. That world is gone, my friend.

Today, our world involves us becoming beyond frustrated when we receive a phone call that wasn't planned, when we receive too many texts at once, or our smartphone's Internet takes an extra second to load a page. *This says a lot about how we have evolved as consumers and about what we expect from the outside world.*

What are we currently doing wrong?

With the enormous growth of sales positions, independent contractors, and entrepreneurs, a huge disconnect on how to sell has been created. If you log in to any social media site, you'll see numerous people posting a link to their product or service, asking you to buy it. *Why should you?* If you're one of these people who simply post a link and expect to make sales: Why are you doing it? What are your current sales like? Are you building long-term relationships? Unless you're a celebrity, influencer, or have an endorsement, people probably aren't listening to you. *You are interrupting the conversation.*

What do I mean when by that? Anyone on social media who *isn't* selling something is there to engage with others. They are literally having a conversation. When you post a salesy status or make an unrelated comment, it falls in the middle of conversations that are already happening—and it brings those discussions to a halt. Stop selling to us like you're a billboard and we're driving past you. You've posted your sales pitch loud and clear: "READ THIS COPY: NOW BUY THIS PRODUCT."

This is *not* the way sales is done. *Selling on social media does not mean you take your print ad and post it on a social media profile.*

If you're not publicly interrupting the conversation, you're still whispering things that only I can hear, *but I still don't want to hear them.* You do this by sending me messages. I receive new LinkedIn connection requests and Facebook friend requests every single day, and I accept almost all of them. I give everyone an opportunity to swing the bat if they want—or to come in, watch what I'm doing, and see what I have to say. I receive messages every single day from people wanting me to buy their products or services. I can tell if you've copied and pasted a script and you send it to everyone with whom you connect with. You've asked to connect with me but haven't said a word to me. You've provided zero value to me, and now you're asking me to buy from you?

When was the last time you bought something from a stranger on social media because he or she sent you only a link to their product or service?

Where to Begin: Your Foundation

Before you start creating a marketing and selling strategy, ask yourself the following questions.

1. Am I selling or promoting myself or my company?

This may sound strange at first, but let's look a little deeper. If you've been a mortgage broker with a couple of different companies, you may want to mainly focus on selling yourself. You want to be known as the hardworking, reliable, and trustworthy person, regardless of with which company you're working. If that business folds, or you move to another city, the people you worked with might not remember the name of the company, but they *will* remember you. If they're connected with you on a social platform, have your e-mail, or at a bare minimum have your phone number, they'll call *you* first because *you* built that relationship. You're able to evolve and adapt. Don't rely on a company you don't own to do that for you.

If you own this company, you can sell and market yourself differently. You're able to promote the company as a whole.

2. *How much money am I budgeting for advertising?*

Advertising doesn't have to be expensive. You can be effective online while spending *nothing* if you spend your time correctly. If you do have a budget, you're able to reach your target audience at a much faster and less tedious rate. If you can find a budget for advertising, put those dollars to work in the most effective and efficient ways possible.

3. *Who is my target market?*

If you're not able to clearly define this, you'll spend a lot of money, time, and effort going in a number of directions. In the end, you'll be unhappy with the results. *No one* can afford to target everyone. If your target markets are "parents," "business owners," or "homeowners," that market is too broad. You may be asking, "How do I determine who my target market is?" Start by examining your customer base. Who currently uses your products? Look for common characteristics among your customers. If you're a brand-new company that hasn't yet established a customer base, look at your competition. Is there another company similar to yours that does extremely well? Who do they target? Who uses their products? Look at their audience and see if you can identify common characteristics. Let your competitor do the hard work of identifying a target market; then you can simply follow suit. Don't stop there, though. Are there small areas your competition overlooks? Is there a niche they're missing?

You've probably heard that you need to find out the demographics of your customer base. This includes but is not limited to age, gender, marital status, location, income, and education level. This is helpful for narrowing down your target audience, but you should also think about the psychographics—the lifestyle, hobbies, personalities, and interests—of your customers. Why should you know these things? Because you need to make sure whatever product or service you're selling fits into your target customer's life.

Note: Defining a target market does not mean that people outside of the market won't be reached or possibly turn into customers. You are just putting an emphasis on where the majority of your business comes from.

4. What platform(s) does my target market use?

Once you've determined your target market, find out where their eyes and ears regularly go. I've seen a trend of businesses and independent contractors that only use the platforms that *they* use to promote their business. If you limit yourself to only those platforms that are convenient to you, you'll miss out on *a lot* of potential sales.

Later in this chapter, we'll cover what I believe are the top three platforms that will increase mortgage sales.

5. What is my end goal? Am I trying to get my business off the ground so people will have heard of us? Am I trying to gain more "likes" on Facebook? Or am I just trying to stay relevant?

The only way to determine if a marketing campaign works is to have an end goal in mind. Make it a clear and specific goal. If you're a brand-new company and want to build your audience on LinkedIn, you could set goals for a specific quantity and quality of connections. You can publish daily posts and run the analytics to discover who is viewing them.

Your goal can be as simple as you'd like. A good example of a specific goal is aiming to gain a thousand new likes on your Facebook page by running a $50 giveaway campaign for one week. Just be clear so you have something by which to judge the performance of your campaign.

6. Am I capable of doing these things myself, or do I need to hire someone?

Hopefully after you've read this book, you'll be able to do most of the hard work yourself. But if you're, for example, putting together a video that needs editing, music, and more—and this is outside of your expertise—ask a friend if they can help you out. Don't spend dollars just to spend them. If you're unable to do something and aren't willing to learn or don't have the necessary tools, first ask your network of friends and colleagues for help. If you come up empty-handed, you may need to hire someone.

Getting into the Nitty-Gritty

Now that we've built a foundation and know what *not* to do, let's break down each platform to ensure we're using it correctly. There are three main social platforms that will greatly benefit mortgage brokers: Meetup, Facebook, and LinkedIn, each of which is used for different purposes. The ways in which I speak to my family, friends, co-workers, and bosses all differ. In the same way, the ways in which you communicate on each platform should be different. Each site has its own language; just because something works well on social media platform does not mean it can be used identically on another platform and yield the same results. Some prefer pictures over text and hashtags over long copy. Posting the most well-said quote in a world of videos won't get you the results you want.

In the words of Gary Vaynerchuk, "If content is king, then context is God."

Meetup

Meetup connects people in a specific area to get together for, you guessed it, a Meetup. What is a Meetup? According to the website, "Meetups are neighbors getting together to learn something, do something, or share something."

Start by either going to the website or downloading the application on your phone. I prefer using the app due to its simplicity. The point of Meetup isn't the online interaction; instead, it's connecting with people in your locale face-to-face. Meetup gives you the ability to see what's going on in your community. Meetups are fantastic for local businesses and salespeople to get their names into the community. I've even seen great success when used by orthopedic surgeons (I'll describe that shortly).

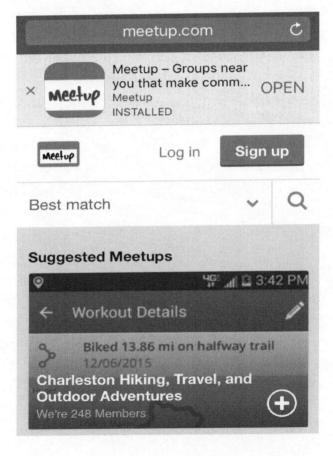

How often do you go outside of your comfort zone and meet new people? It can be intimidating showing up somewhere to meet people with whom you've had no interaction. You don't have to go alone, though. Bring a friend!

When you look for local Meetups, you'll see a lot of them dealing with networking, small business, entrepreneurs, etc. But I'm not asking you to go to solely networking meetings. You're probably thinking, "This is a book on selling . . . why *wouldn't* I only attend these?" When I first started using Meetup, these were the only events I joined, and there was absolutely no change in my sales—not after day one or month six. When you attend networking Meetups, you'll soon realize they're composed of all the same people. What sort of people? People who want to sell their products or services. That is their only goal, and for the most part, they don't have any interest in what you have to say. They provide zero value. I recommend becoming a member of one of these networking groups in the event that there are people with whom you can directly work and who have reliable referral sources. The perfect networking Meetup group is one that is newly formed and free so you can be a part of the group's building process—and so you can be the person who comes to mind when someone asks a group member for a referral.

What other Meetups should you attend? This shouldn't be difficult to answer. Be active in Meetups in which you truly have interest. When on the Meetup app, you're asked to create a profile, share a little bit about yourself, and choose your interests from a list. When personalizing these options, you can click on "Calendar" and see relevant Meetups under "My Meetups & Suggestions." There are Meetups related to everything from kayaking and hiking, to board games and reading, to food lovers and drinking.

Earlier, I mentioned a friend of mine who is an orthopedic surgeon specializing in foot and ankle injuries. He has great success using Meetups to enhance his business. He attends *zero* networking Meetups. He only goes to Meetups having to do with physical activities such as kickball, dodgeball, and flag football. Every season, he makes new friends and participates in fun sports, and when someone sprains their ankle, they go and see him! Brilliant! Find out how you can incorporate both fun and business into attending Meetups.

Not having luck with your current Meetups suggestions? If you want to search everything and not be limited to what's recommended specifically for you, go to "Calendar" and select "All Meetups nearby."

The more you get involved, the more connections you'll make outside of your usual circle. You'll build relationships and grow your business on a local and personal level!

Don't go to these events and simply ask people for their business. As we discussed earlier in this chapter, you must first provide value. Introduce yourself and stay on topic. As you become an active, regular member, people will want to know more about you. This is when you let them know who you are, what you do professionally, and what else you're involved in around town. As you make friends, they'll likely add you on LinkedIn, Facebook, Instagram, and whatever other social media platforms they use. They'll see what you're doing and posting. You'll create a connection without *ever* having to put on your "sales face."

Facebook

Facebook allows you to have a presence no matter where your company is located and regardless of what you're selling. Unlike social media platforms used in the past, Facebook is changing with consumers' needs while also creating and steering us toward things we didn't even realize we wanted. Its algorithm has shown success by putting everything we want right in front of our eyes. It is becoming a one-stop shop for accessing the entire world. In this section, I'll go into exact detail regarding how to maximize your time, money, engagement, and value on Facebook.

Marketers are finally realizing Facebook isn't a fad and it has a huge upside for targeting your exact market. Facebook isn't showing any signs of slowing down, either. In December of 2012, there were just over a one billion monthly active users. On August 27, 2015, they announced one billion active users in a *single day*.[1]

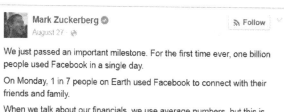

Mark Zuckerberg
August 27 ·

We just passed an important milestone. For the first time ever, one billion people used Facebook in a single day.

On Monday, 1 in 7 people on Earth used Facebook to connect with their friends and family. [2]

When we talk about our financials, we use average numbers, but this is different. This was the first time we reached this milestone, and it's just the beginning of connecting the whole world.

I'm so proud of our community for the progress we've made. Our community stands for giving every person a voice, for promoting understanding and for including everyone in the opportunities of our modern world.

A more open and connected world is a better world. It brings stronger relationships with those you love, a stronger economy with more opportunities, and a stronger society that reflects all of our values.

Thank you for being part of our community and for everything you've done to help us reach this milestone. I'm looking forward to seeing what we accomplish together.

So you want to market your company on Facebook? Let's start by doing so on a "free" level, and we'll work our way up the ladder to more advanced strategies. I use quotation marks around the word "free" because

1 "Company Info," *Facebook*, last modified September 30, 2015, https://newsroom.fb.com/company-info/.

2 *Facebook*, last modified August 27, 2015, https://www.facebook.com/zuck/posts/10102329188394581.

while you need to spend zero dollars, you will need to spend time.

I quickly realized that posting *everything* mortgage-related on my profile didn't make sense unless I was licensed in all fifty states. Now ask yourself: Are all your friends *really* your target market? If you answered no, then you need to set up a Facebook Page, which is simple to do.

While signed in to Facebook on your computer, go to the top right of the page and click the drop-down arrow. A couple of lines down, you'll see "Create Page." Click on this; then, you'll see a set of different pages from which to choose.

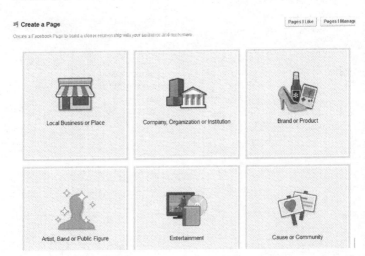

Select the type of page that is relevant to what you'd like to build. If you're promoting yourself as a mortgage broker, you may want to choose "Artist, Band, or Public Figure" and specify that you're a public figure. If you own the business, choosing "Company, Organization or Institution" will likely be more appropriate. Once you select your page type, you can choose the category in which your page bests belongs, and then you can also specify what you'd like to name your page. Once this is completed, you'll be prompted to enter a description about your business, add a profile picture, and target an audience!

Set Up Insert Beauty BRAND HERE

| 1 About | 2 Profile Picture | 3 Add to Favorites | 4 Preferred Page Audience |

Tip: Add a description and website to improve the ranking of your Page in search.
Fields marked by asterisks (*) are required.

Add a few sentences to tell people what your Page is about. This will help it show up in the right search results. You will be able to add more details later from your Page settings.

155

*Tell people what your Page is about

Website (ex: your website, Twitter or other social media links)

Need Help?   Skip   Save Info

The benefits of being able to target your audience are huge. If you're a mortgage broker licensed in one state and don't have an online selling platform—just a brick-and-mortar shop—you'll obviously want to direct your posts to people in your region. Alternately, if you're licensed in several or all states, choose the locations you want to target. Along with choosing the location, you can specify the interests of your target audience. Not sure what to pick? Next to "Interests," there is a button you can click for suggestions based off what you've already entered about your page; you're also provided with the number of people who have "liked" pages related to that particular interest. Facebook completely takes the guess-work out for you.

Now that you've created your page, you're all set! Facebook takes you through a quick tutorial on how to use the page. Follow along with it to familiarize yourself with your page's layout.

After your page is created and spruced up with images and your first post, go to your personal profile and publish a post saying something along the lines of: "Thank you to everyone for supporting my business so far! To keep my professional and personal lives separate, I've created a Facebook page *just* for my business. You can find it right here: [insert page's URL]. I'd also like to avoid spamming you; I apologize for all the business-related posts you've read and maybe rolled your eyes at."

You'll automatically get respect for moving your business-related posts to a page and your Facebook friends who like your new page can provide you with direct insight into how you're doing and what you may want to do differently.

You've created a page and have informed your Facebook friends . . . now what do you do? You post things! But remember: We aren't posting "Buying a home? Call me" ads. You need to offer valuable posts to your followers.

Examples of good posts:

- Links to real estate articles

- Quick updates about changes happening in the industry

- Answers to questions you frequently receive, either in video or text format

- Information about events going on around town (not everything has to be mortgage related)

- High-quality pictures and videos

With your page, you're able to post in a much more efficient way. Facebook pages allow you to create a post and schedule when you'd like it to be published on your page. After you've created the post, instead of clicking "Publish," click the drop-down arrow, which provides the option to save the draft, backdate it, or schedule it for publication.

Let's say you've started posting and notice little to no engagement. Why? Lack of followers, lack of engagement on your part? Maybe both? Let's break down how to change it.

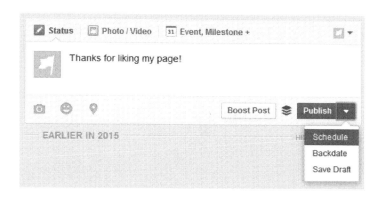

Lack of Followers

If you're posting great information but have no audience, you'll have no results. This is where Facebook says, "You have to pay to play." The most effective way I've found to accumulate followers is by offering a small gift. Following is my campaign in its entirety so you can steal whichever parts you believe can work for you.

Campaign goal: Increase page likes and overall awareness

Offer: Four free tickets to a local festival—$39 value

Target market: Anyone thirty years of age or older living within twenty-five miles of Charleston, South Carolina

Run time: 6:00 a.m.–11:00 p.m. EST for six days straight

Budget: $200

FREE 4-PACK TICKET GIVEAWAY!!

How to enter:
1. Share this post
2. Like our page

Winner announced this Tuesday! GOOD LUCK CHARLESTONIANS!

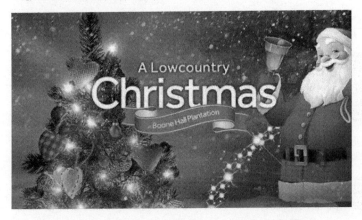

1,184 Likes · 289 Comments · 1,862 Shares

👍 Like | 💬 Comment | ➦ Share

Notice that the call to action is incredibly simple: like the page and share the post, which provides us with free advertising.

Audience

Gender	Age	Placement ▼

LIFETIME RESULTS

Women

Post Engagements	2,586
Cost per Post Engagement	$0.07
Reached	31,358

Men

Post Engagements	156
Cost per Post Engagement	$0.14
Reached	6,656

As you can see, female engagement for this particular post was off the charts!

Audience

Gender	Age	Placement ▼

LIFETIME RESULTS

Desktop News Feed

Post Engagements	37
Cost per Post Engagement	$0.09
Reached	1,626

Mobile News Feed

Post Engagements	2,712
Cost per Post Engagement	$0.07
Reached	36,924

From the above, it's clear that mobile has become the most common way to access information. If what you post does not function on mobile devices, change your plan immediately

To build your own simple campaign post boost, follow these steps (from a computer):

1. After you create a post, click on the drop-down arrow at the top right of your Facebook page.

2. Click "Create Ads."

3. Click "Boost your posts."

4. Choose the post you'd like to boost.

5. Click "Set Audience & Budget."

6. At the top of the page, everything you choose will be specific to you: where you live and who you'd like to target for purchasing a home, refinancing, and everything in between.

7. Choose if you'd like to run the ad daily or for a certain period of time.

8. Determine your budget. I recommend creating several ads, using different target markets, running each ad for a week, and use the same small budget for each ad. This will allow you to learn more about your active audience before betting large and going all in.

9. The final page lets you customize your text. Make sure there is a defined call to action.

10. On this page, you can also choose where your ad appears. From my experiences, the right side of the page, when viewed on a computer, is obsolete. Even if your target market is in their sixties and seventies, chances are they still use Facebook on a mobile device.

11. When complete, simply click "Place order."

You have now placed an ad! It can take anywhere from a minute to twenty-four hours for your ad to be approved. Then you can track your results on a mobile device and/ or your computer. If you see dollars go to waste in certain areas, you can edit the ad at any time, or you can turn it off completely and reevaluate your campaign.

Lack of Engagement

Now that you have a page, make sure you're not only talking—you need to listen as well. What does that entail? Start by liking relevant pages, whether they relate to the mortgage industry, local businesses, media outlets, neighborhood groups, etc. Use these pages to interact with others. Share things these pages post to show your support, comment on posts, and ultimately get your name out to even more Facebook users. Engaging on social media costs nothing; you simply have to put forth effort and spend time doing it.

Facebook allows us to connect to almost everyone in the world with minimal effort. *Do not* overlook Facebook when it comes to building your brand via social media. Create a page, build it, engage with and attract followers, and post the right content. The value you provide will be what makes someone choose you over the mortgage broker next door.

LinkedIn

The final social site we'll discuss is LinkedIn. This platform isn't ideal for all industries and sometimes doesn't even make sense to spend time on. For a mortgage broker, it is a great outlet to gain referral sources. Unlike Facebook, where your main audience is the general population, LinkedIn should be used specifically for connecting with Realtors, developers, and builders.

Let's start from the beginning. . . . Log in or sign up with LinkedIn and start with the basics. Make sure you complete the following immediately:

- Profile picture
- Summary
- Education
- Work experience
- Hobbies and interests

LinkedIn is a professional platform, so make sure your posts are professional. This means no selfies as your profile picture and no YouTube videos that show complete immaturity. We judge a book by its cover. *This*, my friend, is your cover. How you interact with others and what you post are the pages in between.

Key ingredients for the perfect LinkedIn profile are:

Posting Updates

Similarly to Facebook, posting updates on LinkedIn won't garner much attention or engagement because those updates can slide down the newsfeed quickly and get lost. If you only have a sentence or quick rant to share, post an update and tag someone with whom you recently discussed it or who would appreciate and possibly relate with what you've said.

Publishing Posts

If you have something to share that could be in a blog post or article format, publish a post. With a post, you can choose a header picture, use tags to make it easier to find, and share it to all your social media platforms. After it's been up for a day, you can look at the post's analytics to see where your traffic is coming from. You can see the professions of those reading your post, what site they came to your post from, and where they live.

Connections

Being connected with others on LinkedIn is the only way people will know you exist and will be able to see what you're saying. When you're trying to build up a base of connections, start by connecting with people you know, either personally or professionally. When you first sign in, LinkedIn's algorithms will suggest individuals you may know who are also on LinkedIn. After that, your list of "People you may know" could be filled entirely with strangers. Once you get to this point, there is a tactical way to continue adding people.

We're in the mortgage business and want to connect with Realtors, developers, and builders. At the top of every LinkedIn page, you can search by profession. The resulting list will contain the most relevant people, some of whom might be connected to you through another connection (who could possibly introduce you); others may just be in your geographic area. When connecting with strangers on LinkedIn, it's vital to send them a personalized message after they've accepted your request to connect. Let them know you're a mortgage broker in town and are trying to connect with like-minded individuals. If they post things you like, engage and let them know! Alternately, when someone connects with you on LinkedIn, take thirty seconds out of your day to send them a personalized message.

Groups

Like Meetup, LinkedIn has groups. They can be focused on happy hours, alumni associations, networking, job searching, new residents, and a plethora of other topics. Join several groups and be active within them. When you post in a group, members who aren't connected with you will see your post. If you share something engaging, it will bring attention to you and your business.

LinkedIn is simple to use, there is no cost for using their basic platform, and all you're expected to do is give up some of your time to engage with your audience.

With everyone's heads buried in their phones, it simply doesn't make sense for you to lack an online presence. Don't use these platforms to sell, sell, sell, and push your services. Use them instead as a place to share knowledge from which you believe others will benefit. Through online communication and engagement, you'll increase awareness, establish trust, and ultimately boost your sales.

6

Competing with
the Banks

W HEN I STARTED as a mortgage broker, one of the
very first questions I asked my future employer
was, "How do I compete with area bank loan officers?"
Without hesitation, he said, "Very simple. You beat them
on price!" That should be magic to any salesperson's
ears, as the ability to out-price the competition is one of
the best advantages an individual can possibly have,
regardless of what he or she is selling. If you can offer a
lower price—or, in our case, a lower rate—you have a
great advantage. Walmart uses a price advantage model,
and that seems to work out very well for them. I've heard
a mortgage broker described as having the Sam's Club or
Costco of rates; that's true in the sense that we have lower
prices in the form of lower rates. This is the absolute key
advantage we have over any brick-and-mortar bank with

whom you'll compete. In most cases, the lowest rate will win the deal.

Any local bank will have higher operating costs in the form of tellers, maintaining a brick-and-mortar location, ATMs–everything right on down to the deposit slips. None of these things appear on a mortgage broker's ledger.

I regularly check the local larger banks' rates so I know what we may or may not be competing with in the market. With my warehouse line, I act as my own secondary marketing department, so I can control the price we put on any deal. At any given time, we are usually 0.125 to 0.25 percent better than the banks in rate, and with a larger difference in price. Also keep in mind that the bank loan officer has zero control over the price the bank puts out there.

Be aware that the correspondent model is similar to a bank model, so you may not have the same pricing advantage. Make sure your margins are set correctly so you can keep that advantage in place. My setup as a broker and lender allows me to use my advantage when necessary. Especially keep this in mind if you are setting up your own shop. A mini-correspondent takes on the risk of having the loan on his or her warehouse line as an intermediary. This means that a mini-correspondent will earn a service release premium (SRP). By taking the extra steps and capital requirements to become a mini-correspondent, you can have this pricing advantage available to you at all times.

For a six-month period, I was with a regional bank, and I couldn't get out of there fast enough after hearing some "logic" from the upper levels. At the time, we were seeing a minor rate dip that led to some refinance activity. I still had access to the brokerage side of the industry, including the rate sheets for wholesale investors. I noticed that my new employer's rate was roughly 0.25 percent higher than everyone else's, so I asked a simple question: "Why are our rates so bad?" The answer I got was less than encouraging. The senior vice president of mortgage told me that underwriting and processing were backed up, so they increased the rate to stop the flow of production to avoid creating a bottleneck. Needless to say, I found an excuse to run into my former employer, who wanted to get me back and offered me a promotion. So the stars had aligned, and I got out of that bank as fast as I could. It's not that I think banks are bad places to work—it's that as a frontline salesperson, you're only as good as the rate you offer. Knowing that banks would increase their rates to make them less competitive isn't necessarily a great thing for the bank loan officer, who's competing on a daily basis. Add to that the lower compensation models most banks are adopting to improve their own bottom line, and I wouldn't look to sign back up to the world of big banks any time . . . ever. To the banks' own end, they have turned their business into an impersonal numbers game. Keep in mind that these same bankers are themselves a referral source for the business they can't handle due to their higher standards.

A local mortgage broker should also use the niche and expanded product offerings to his or her advantage, as the conservative approach taken by most banks will create a segment of the population that doesn't fit the bank model. Currently we are seeing a new offering of products including bank statement programs; programs for those with past foreclosures, short sales, or bankruptcy; and programs for investors. One of the more creative programs to come out is an investor cash flow program geared towards people constantly buying homes that looks at the actual or potential cash flow of the property. The cash flow of a property is simply how much the property can rent for on any given month. Whatever the home makes is written off of your debts and allows you to move on to the next home to purchase. The main factor that sets these products apart is that the investors require significantly more capital in terms of a down payment. This increase in collateral further secures these loans, making it so the borrower has something significant to lose should he or she try to walk away. A terrific resource to keep up with new product lines and offerings is the Scotsman Guide—particularly their index of lender options. It is the best industry-related guide for mortgage brokers out there.

A good mortgage broker should mean more lending options and great rates.

Finding Your Niche

G IVEN THE HURDLES that now must be jumped before entering our industry, the sooner new loan officers or mortgage brokers can find their niche, the sooner they'll see success. This challenge can be overcome with a little bit of direction and a lot of effort. The sooner you can find a common ground with your target market, the sooner you can get results in the form of direct referrals.

Let's take a look at some potential referral source niches you can approach. I'll break them into two basic groups: exclusive niche and open niche. The exclusive niche requires some type of membership or common ground from past experience. For example, if you are a military veteran, then servicing other veterans with VA loans is an exclusive niche. While any loan officer can sell a VA loan, veterans may feel more comfortable with another veteran walking them through the home-buying process. Every individual and group in society has a niche. Not all are as valuable as others in terms of mortgages, but that's why we have open niches, which can either be joined or purchased.

In terms of exclusive niches, let's take a look at some potential methods of entry.

1. VA or Military Borrowers

A natural fit for anyone who has served our country. There are numerous companies that only issue VA leads. You can also join charity efforts related to service vets or take advantage of membership opportunities at establishments like your local VFW.

2. Alumni Associations

These are very big, especially in the South, with colleges that have athletic support groups and alumni associations. If you don't have one in your area, then by all means start one! A simple method would be to create a regular meeting time around, for example, Indiana basketball games. Appoint a time and location, and get the word out via online message boards. This allows a transplant to grow a local group organically.

Joining a group or association will require you to put in the hours. I mean that literally; many groups already have older members in our industry. You may be the "new guy" when you join the group, but make it known that you're there and willing to participate.

3. Demographic Groups

This would be your friends who are around your age and who have a similar background. At some point, most Americans will buy a home. If you are a mortgage professional of the same age as the people you typically associate yourself with, you will see different purchases at different times throughout their lifetime. Typically, people buy three to five homes in their lifetime.

The first is a starter home. This type of purchase will have a lower cost, may have some type of government backing such as the FHA or the United States Department of Agriculture (USDA) and is geared to a new buyer. The second home is generally the step-up home. This type of property is oftentimes costlier than the starter home and tends to be purchased by people who have just married and plan ahead for kids. The determining factors in a second-home purchase may be geared more toward the quality of the school district and the actual size of the home. Generally, the third purchase would be a trophy home. The buyer for this home is typically in the age group of mid-thirties to late forties. The home is typically a pinnacle or step-up property of larger value. This buyer demographic is at peak earning and oftentimes has experience with property and may be looking at this as the "show" property or as an equity play for later in life. The fourth type of home purchase can potentially come from this age group as well; this fourth purchase is generally investment property or a second home. The final home in a typical person's cycle is the step-down or downsized home, and this purchase is generally made by buyers as they retire, when the kids leave home, or to capitalize on equity. All of this isn't to say that you won't see people make these types of home purchases at different times; this is just a general rule of thumb.

As a loan officer, you can gear your marketing toward those in your age group. A younger loan officer will likely see more first-time buyers, while a seasoned broker may see more trophy or step-down home purchases. Your friends and circle of influence may cross over some, but for the most part, you will deal with customers in demographics similar to yours, so it's important to focus your efforts on these groups. If young loan officers play their cards right, they could ride the aforementioned cycle through multiple purchases from the same buyers as the cycle goes on.

4. Product Specialists

We are starting to see more and more reverse mortgage specialists. This would fall in line with a marketing plan geared toward an older demographic, as reverse mortgages are only for individuals over the age of sixty-two. I tend to believe that an older loan officer will have an easier time selling reverse mortgages due to age.

There have been rumors of pending regulations on reverse mortgages since there are currently many larger commissions being paid, so it is important to keep an eye on regulations. Reverse mortgages have a handful of industry investors you must use, the largest being American Advisors Group (AAG).

There are other examples of product specialists including construction lending and specifically FHA 203(k) lending. For the first example, having a good construction product is paramount, and given the changes caused by TRID, construction loans as a wholesale product will be more difficult to sell and disclose. The 203(k) product is also a unique option that depends on the quality of your investor. This product became harder to sell with the changes made in October 2015. Start educating yourself on becoming a product specialist and incorporate it into your business.

5. Term Niche

Create a term niche for yourself in your market. A new spin could be to present yourself with a more aggressive term—say, a twenty-, fifteen-, or ten-year product. The advantage would be that your rates would in all likelihood be much lower than the industry standard thirty-year fixed rate. The downside is that not everyone will qualify for a lower term with <u>debt-to-income ratio (DTI)</u> limits, so it becomes more important to ensure that you pitch this product to the right demographic. I see this as a more viable option for someone with higher earning power or someone who wants to pay off their mortgage sooner.

6. USDA Consumers

With some effort and gas mileage, this product can be of great value to a mortgage broker. USDA marketing typically needs to be done in person with smaller realty businesses and direct marketing to consumers using zip codes. The key is to market in areas where these homes and properties are located—typically outside of urban areas.

7. Internet Leads

This niche will only be successful if you are consistent with purchasing and working these leads. Once you have a database of significant size, you have a market. Keep in mind that most Internet leads have a shelf life of a few weeks to a few months, but if you are dedicated, have automated your marketing efforts, and maintain campaigns that promote top-of-mind awareness, you should see future returns.

Another option is to partner with Bankrate or LendingTree to garner online leads. I will caution that the profit margins on these lines of business and partnerships can get pretty thin. The good news is most of the consumers are A-paper conventional deals.

8. Direct Mail

As a niche, this is a cost-effective way to build a database and close deals. I have focused primarily on FHA streamlines and converts from FHA to conventional loans. The mail service we use also provides us with lead data so you know you're marketing to a database dedicated to leads for a specific loan type. As rates increase, you may have to change up the variety of mailers that you send, instead promoting other loan types such as HARP, <u>debt consolidation</u>, or ARM conversions.

Be sure to copy the data you get from your mailing service provider into your database. This sounds simple, but lacking to do so is a common mistake: Many loan officers pay for these leads, and then don't have the data for regular follow-up and further marketing. Direct mail is an easy way to get your phone ringing from the right people. Use it!

9. Bankers and Financial Advisors

Bankers are a great referral source, especially in today's market, while they have higher credit score requirements and less flexibility. Most bankers I've met will send referrals your way if you consistently ask them to do so, and if you share information about the products you have in place to service bank customers.

Financial advisors are also a source to consider since most are primarily focused on their clients' goals. In most cases, if you can free up cash flow for a client through refinancing, a strong financial advisor will see that as money they could invest on their client's behalf.

I would also classify certified public accountants (CPAs) as a minor source for referrals, as well as commercial bankers or commercial brokers.

10. First-Time Homebuyers

This niche works well when you can build a seminar-based partnership with a Realtor. Typically, you can attract FHA-type buyers by conducting a seminar with a Realtor, who will promote it to his or her leads. Loan officers who go this route should have strong public speaking skills and be ready for a lot of questions. You need to be well versed in your products and topics to pull these seminars off with success, but it's a referral method that can attract a lot of potential buyers.

11. Divorce Attorneys

When wedded bliss comes to an end, it's time to divide the assets, and that often means one of the individuals leaving the property. Divorce decrees often lead to a refinance in order to remove a person from the obligations associated with former marital assets. Hand out cards to divorce attorneys and be on the lookout for referrals to their clients in needs of lending services.

12. Community or Subdivision Marketing

Typically this works best in high-end markets. This niche requires community involvement and direct marketing to specific zip codes or subdivisions. Realtors do this type of marketing frequently, and a joint marketing campaign may be a good idea to jump-start becoming an area's lender of choice.

13. Spanish-Speaking Buyers

This obviously requires that you speak Spanish; it's a viable and underserved part of many communities. In my experiences, the language barrier keeps Spanish-speaking buyers on the other side of the fence, but once you break down that barrier, you'll see significant results if the population base is large enough. Be aware that there are many programs for buyers with visas, permanent resident alien cards, and/or Individual Tax Identification Numbers (ITINs).

14. Foreign Nationals

This group requires some initial legwork to get the necessary lenders set up and crossing into some associations or market segments. Depending on your location, you may not come across many of these types of loans. Having a background with a community group or some sphere of influence that crosses over into foreign national groups is key to drumming up business this way.

15. Leads Groups

There are numerous leads groups in every market, and most limit their members to include a single representative per industry. The biggest part of participating in a leads group is to offer referrals to other group members.

It will likely be harder to join a leads group versus starting one yourself. A good core group for beginning would include a Realtor, an insurance agent, an advertising salesperson, and any other top-end salesperson. The idea is to fill your group with people who have similar drives and interests in growing their businesses.

16. Blogging and Social Media

Create your own sphere of influence via blogging or active social media use. What will help you most is a top-of-mind awareness among your friends and family—if you remember to ask them to send prospective buyers your way. One of the biggest mistakes young loan officers make with this method is forgetting to ask for business. While blogging and social media can be fun, if you really want to use it professionally, don't get distracted and forget to actually ask for business.

17. Past Clients

Successful closings mean happy clients; one of the best referral sources you can create is your base of past clients. You need a dedicated approach and marketing campaign to establish top-of-mind awareness. Keeping your name in front of previous buyers requires action. Conduct a yearly mortgage review with past clients and use this opportunity as the platform to cross-sell and to ask for referrals. You have to be direct if you want to see results. By making a yearly annual review part of your sales approach, you have the opportunity to reach out for referrals, and you'll also be keeping in touch with them for potential future sales.

18. Realtors

Realtors are the most obvious niche for referrals, but also require the most legwork and the highest level of accountability. Once you work with Realtors and their clients, you can build lasting relationships and referral sources that will continue for the lifetime of your business.

They're so important that they get the entire next chapter of this book...

Doing Business with Realtors in Today's Market

THERE HAS BEEN a lot written about how to best work with Realtors, but I'd like to take it a step further and focus on working with Realtors given the recent changes with TRID. Let's put the spotlight on some of the changes that occurred in October 2015 and how to move forward.

If you aren't in our industry, it would be beneficial for us to first discuss TRID, which is an acronym created by combining two other mortgage-related acronyms: the Truth in Lending Act (TILA) and the Real Estate Settlement Procedures Act (RESPA). TRID is the marriage of these acts into a final order for further disclosure to the consumer. Based upon initial returns, I can tell you that it's a painful change for Realtors, closing attorneys, and now the consumer. In terms of what those in our industry have been facing, I think the attitude has been that this is just more of the same. The Consumer Financial Protection Board (CFPB) combined the acts into one ruling that changed some of the disclosures we use with consumers.

How does this relate to Realtors? Simply put, it raises the bar for everyone on a communication level, and now any third-party fees that weren't properly disclosed via a loan estimate as well as any changes must be disclosed to the consumer. All of these disclosures lead to the most important part of the ruling, which is the Closing Disclosure (CD) form. The client must be given the correct final CD form to begin a mandatory three-day waiting period. These three days include all days of the week except Sundays and any holiday. For example, if a client accepts the CD on a Thursday, assuming there are no holidays, the earliest the loan can be closed would be Tuesday. If any changes are made to the CD, a new seventy-two-hour waiting period is required.

For mortgage brokers, this once again presents an opportunity to provide leadership to our clients and the Realtors involved in the transactions. As the owner of my company, I now call each Realtor after confirming the CD with my clients. An important aspect of the CD is that the client accepts it either electronically or in person to begin the window. With our clients' permission, at that point I reach out to everyone involved in the closing process. The Realtors aren't copied in unless we reach out to them, and one thing we discovered early on was that the closing attorney didn't always get a copy of the CD from the investor.

I use this as an opportunity to take the lead, go over the CD, and set clear expectations for the closing. Most struggles come from the attorneys; for them, this is a new level of compliance, and they have trust accounts for dispersing the involved loans. I can see and hear the frustration on their end most of all, and I think if brokers take the lead, we can guide everyone through this process.

What I see and hear is that for the majority of lenders, this is just more of the same. We've frequently seen this type of delay in the last five years. First, it was the change of circumstance forms and the delays they could cause if there was a rate change. Then we had to deal with delays caused by appraisal management companies coming in, disclosures for the appraisals, and whether or not our client waived the three-day waiting period. This has all been built into our process for the last few years. For the most part, these delays occurred in the middle of the process and could be built into our interest rate locks already in place and worked into the process.

As an industry, we all now face a delay at the *end* of the process, and this is the key. Previously, Realtors and clients were rarely affected by the delays. The appraisal three-day waiver clause didn't often come into play, and we brokers discovered it was easier to have the client waive this option up-front. TRID is not something that can be waived. I personally don't think seventy-two hours is necessary and I hope at some point that time is reduced, but I can understand the thought process: It gives the closing attorney time to prepare once the client approves the final CD. As brokers, we need to grasp this chance to ensure everyone is on track and knows what to expect and to lead everyone to the closing table.

I would recommend that all brokers use this time to establish themselves as skilled professionals and to set up future sales. By effectively communicating the CD to your clients and Realtors, you present yourself as an expert. The CD's format is uniform and it's a tale of the tape on the transaction, so it creates a setup that's ideal for you to flow into the numbers and hit some high points.

The closing information on the CD will include the date the documents were prepared and will outline the dates for closing and disbursement. Obviously, it will show if you delivered the transaction in under thirty days, allowing you to prepare the necessary information and avoid delays. The transaction and loan information documents are in an easy-to-read format. The next items on the CD are the interest rate and payment options. This is when you should highlight the rates you were able to procure for the client and, if necessary, go over the specific scenario, highlighting the rate. If you were initially competing for the loan, you may want to have notes prepared comparing your rate to the competitors'. It never hurts to highlight the benefits of doing business with you and your company. At the bottom of the CD's first page is a simple-to-decipher breakdown of the closing costs and cash to close. It's important to go over the details again and make sure the Realtor knows you hit your numbers.

The second page is an itemized breakdown of the closing costs and prepaid items. Again, this is a much friendlier format and is easier for the consumer to understand when compared with what we just recently had as a good faith estimate, which I found to be confusing for a layman.

On the third page of the CD, the initial loan estimate is compared with the final numbers. Always be ready to go over any differences; be able to backtrack any changes that were made on the borrower's behalf. For example, if a borrower on a refinance decided to slightly increase his rate to cover more of the closing costs. People don't always remember all the twists and turns their loan may have taken during the process, and that is one of the great things about being required to disclose change to borrowers via a new loan estimate: It creates a record to use later if necessary. Don't think of having to re-disclose the loan estimate as negative; instead, think of it as a tracking log that clearly defines all the transaction's changes. Embrace these documents as a living record for the transaction. If you or your team made mistakes along the way, be ready to go over those items and clearly tell your client how and why the error occurred, as well as what you plan to do to correct it going forward.

The fourth page of the CD is mostly filler; I don't see much reason to dig too deep into the disclosures that were given to the client.

The final page offers the chance to wrap up the transaction by clearly showing the client post-closing contact information they may need, including their lender's info, your name, and the closing agent's information. Above the contact information is a small spot that includes a tax deduction reminder. This is a nice way to wrap up the disclosure: with a friendly reminder that the borrower needs to apply for the 4 percent versus 6 percent mileage rate by listing this property as the primary residence (which will cause lower taxes). Obviously, only tell them to apply for the ratio and tax break if this will be the primary residence. I probably see a half-dozen clients a month who didn't change their taxes and have been overpaying their property taxes for years. I would classify most of them as past first-time homebuyers who never filled out the necessary paperwork. Most first-time homebuyers have never dealt with this item, and if they are purchasing a newly constructed property, this subsection is incredibly relevant. This helps you close the deal by highlighting your expertise and flows nicely with the overall presentation of the CD.

Behind this section, a generic mock loan estimate and CD for a fictional purchase will be attached. These documents are generated from Calyx Point, our operating system, but now that the documents are uniform, they should match up with what everyone is seeing out there across the industry.

TRID has caused changes for everyone in the industry, but in my opinion, it does clean up and offer more user-friendly documents. It helps boil the hundreds of pages related to the process down to three easy-to-read and -understand sheets. Accept this as a positive and clear change that helps you communicate with your borrowers and their Realtors. The sooner you can master them and learn to educate others around you, the sooner you can turn these changes into a new referral source. People are naturally afraid of change; if you can be the one to lead them through these changes, you cement your position as an industry and market expert.

9

How to Use TRID to Your Advantage

As of October 3rd, 2015, we face more disclosure changes, and these items will finally affect the general public. I don't see much benefit to the changes caused by TRID in reference to the timelines they place on items. I see tremendous benefits in the new loan estimates and the eventual ending with CDs.

The CD is the single biggest change; it condenses the numerous pages of paperwork created in the loan-making process into a five-page document. The new CD appears to cause more confusion for closing attorneys. From what I've seen, the larger closing attorneys are picking it up well, but attorneys who do fewer real estate transactions tend to be slower to pick up these changes. If possible, stick with the larger real estate closing firms in your area.

I personally like the CD, as it's much simpler and more precise than the Good Faith Estimate (GFE). I thought the GFE changes after Dodd-Frank came out were terrible. They took a one-page document and turned it into five pages.

The key is communication. Once again, you need to make sure that as soon as a CD is issued by your investor, you get a copy to everyone involved, specifically the closing attorney. My company was already following a process where we'd re-disclose any changes to our clients, so re-disclosing a loan estimate isn't a big deal for us. I can see how an individual broker could have a hard time keeping up, but keep in mind that if you broker your deals, the investor should be taking care of this. We have both lender and broker capabilities, so we have control over our disclosures, which makes re-disclosures easier to accomplish.

The three-day holding period at the end will be the biggest change for consumers and their Realtors. However, I think this waiting period may make closing a loan easier as it becomes more of a part of the transaction. In the grand scheme of things, it should make closings much less dramatic, as what was approved prior to the holding period signifies the end of any changes to the <u>HUD</u>. We as mortgage brokers can use this waiting period to our advantage and see it as another chance to talk and go over terms with your client. Kind of a "mission accomplished" phone call.

The most obvious change for the consumer is this waiting period, and it isn't particularly beneficial. I'm not sure where the idea for a seventy-two-hour waiting period came from. In my mind, this is just an enforcement of a rule that was already on the books. HUDs and settlement statements were always supposed to be given to clients forty-eight hours in advance of closing, but in my fourteen years of experience, I can say that very rarely occurred.

These changes put a lot more pressure on the attorneys and their paralegals to balance everything out with the CD when it's issued, so the loan officer's job becomes quite simple at this point: Make sure everyone is on the same page the second the CD is issued.

As the owner of my company, I personally call each client to go over the CD with them before they even have the chance to see it in their email account. If we have to make any changes, we can then reissue the loan estimate and get everyone on the same page by re-disclosing. I also personally handle all the communication that takes place with our Realtor partners. Most importantly, I personally drive the bus all the way to the finish line for each closing.

If mortgage brokers embrace these changes, they can easily turn TRID into an opportunity to shine through control and knowing about industry changes as they happen. A good mortgage broker can use these disclosures as a way to both close the deal and ask for referrals. If you don't ask for referrals, I can guarantee that you won't receive as many as you deserve.

Summary

THERE HAVE BEEN a lot of changes in our industry since 2008, and not all of them have been good for mortgage brokers. For mortgage brokers to survive and succeed in this new market, they must be able to stay in front of the new rules and take advantage of these changes by becoming fully integrated and having vast knowledge of the new system. Having this expertise will allow us to position ourselves as the go-to lending source for the future. A broker who doesn't embrace these changes will have issues surviving in this marketplace. A mortgage professional who can turn these changes into an opportunity to lead their clients will thrive.

In general, I think we are in a struggle against banks, and the increased regulations challenge us both. The best way to overcome and succeed is to work with likeminded individuals and share information that can help other brokers. Mortgage brokers have received a bad rap the past few years; we all need to move forward together.

I've laid out numerous topics that should be of value to any mortgage broker or mortgage shop owner. If we position ourselves correctly over the next few years, I think we'll see a migration of bankers to our side of the fence. I believe the banks view mortgage professionals as just another part of their machine. Lower compensation will eventually lead bank loan officers to start looking across the fence at the greener grass that mortgage brokerage can offer.

Those brokerage shops that can position themselves for a growth opportunity with the next interest cycle will be set up for a wealth of success. We are currently riding very low rates; as the economy improves, we'll see the rates increase some, allowing for us to have a refinance swing in the next three to five years. Brokers ready to take in experienced loan officers and offer higher compensation than banks will be able to successfully recruit.

An interesting offshoot caused by the increased education requirements and tight regulations is there are fewer new loan officers getting into our industry. I have recently seen fewer applications from college grads than at any point in my career. The new barriers to entry have and will continue to cause a decreased number of new employees over the next few years. I can already see the results of this lack of new blood. The loan officers at the top of the pyramid are getting more and more transactions, and there is less competition from new bodies in the industry. I see this as a good thing in the short term, but we'll need to eventually replenish the ranks. For now, the opportunity exists for seasoned mortgage consultants to capture more and more market share.

The best advice I can give is to build a quality team around you and stay ahead of the curve when it comes to regulations. We can often learn more from adversity than we could from easy success. I have faced my fair share of challenges, and I see light at the end of the tunnel for myself and for our industry. Staying informed and communicating with others facing the same obstacles will help us all succeed in the face of change.

I hope that if nothing else, we've laid out some useful ideas for individuals in our industry. I plan for this to be a series, and I ask that anyone experiencing success who has best practices to share, please contact me directly at Info@JasonCMyers.com. I'd like to have open dialogue and will answer any questions I can from anyone out there who's making their way. Feel free to share what may or may not be working in your market. I would love to share these experiences and triumphs with others in our industry. If I can be of any assistance, by all means reach out to me—I'll respond.

Glossary

Consent order: An agreement between an individual or business and a regulatory body in which the individual or business agrees to pay for damages caused by violations and to cease activities that caused the damages to occur.

Construction lending: A short-term loan used to finance the building of a home or another real estate project. The builder or home buyer takes out a construction loan to cover the costs of the project before obtaining long-term funding. Because they are considered fairly risky, construction loans usually have higher interest rates than traditional mortgage loans.

Consumer Financial Protection Board (CFPB): A regulatory agency charged with overseeing financial products and services that are offered to consumers. The Consumer Financial Protection Bureau is divided into several units, including: research, community affairs, consumer complaints, the Office of Fair Lending and the Office of Financial Opportunity. These units work together to protect and educate consumers about the various types of financial products and services that are available.

Correspondent: The name given to a bank, broker, dealer, or financial institution that acts on behalf of another financial institution with limited or restricted access to the financial markets where a transaction must occur. Commonly done by smaller financial corporations that don't necessarily have the capital to enter into foreign markets and set up new operations. This is a cheaper method of providing international services to clients through agreements and partnerships.

Debt consolidation: The combining of several unsecured debts into a single, new loan that is more favorable. Debt consolidation involves taking out a new loan to pay off a number of other debts. The new loan may result in a lower interest rate, lower monthly payment or both. Consumers can use debt consolidation as a tool to make it easier to get out of student loan debt, credit card debt and other types of debt that aren't tied to an asset.

Debt-to-income ratio (DTI): A personal finance measure that compares an individual's debt payment to his or her overall income. A debt-to-income ratio (DTI) is one way lenders (including mortgage lenders) measure an individual's ability to manage monthly payment and repay debts. DTI is calculated by dividing total recurring monthly debt by gross monthly income, and it is expressed as a percentage. For example, John pays $1,000 each month for his mortgage, $500 for his car loan and $500 for the rest of his debt each month, so his total recurring monthly debt equals $2,000 ($1,000 + $500 + $500). If John's gross monthly income is $6,000, his DTI would be $2,000 ÷ $6,000 = 0.33, or 33%.

Dodd-Frank Wall Street Reform and Consumer Protection Act: A compendium of federal regulations, primarily affecting financial institutions and their customers, that the Obama administration passed in 2010 in an attempt to prevent the recurrence of events that caused the 2008 financial crisis. The Dodd-Frank Wall Street Reform and Consumer

Protection Act, commonly referred to as simply "Dodd-Frank", is supposed to lower risk in various parts of the U.S. financial system. It is named after U.S. Senator Christopher J. Dodd and U.S. Representative Barney Frank because of their significant involvement in the act's creation and passage.

Drip campaign: A strategy employed by many direct marketers where a constant flow of marketing material is sent to customers over a period of time. Drip marketing endeavors to create sales through long-term repeat exposure to its recipients of the goods and services that are advertised.

Federal Housing Association (FHA): A United States government agency that provides mortgage insurance to qualified, FHA-approved lenders. FHA mortgage insurance helps protect lenders from losses associated with mortgage default; if a borrower defaults on a loan, the FHA will pay a specified claim amount to the lender.

FHA 203(k): A type of federally insured mortgage product for individuals who want to rehabilitate or repair a damaged home that will become their primary residence. In addition to the funds to cover the purchase price of the house, the FHA 203(k) loan provides the money needed for repairs and related expenses as part of the loan.

FHA streamline: A mortgage-refinancing option offered by the Federal Housing Administration (FHA). An FHA streamline refinance requires the mortgage to be FHA insured and not delinquent. The refinance must result in a reduction in the home-owner's interest and principal payment, and no cash can be taken out of the refinanced mortgage. There are two forms of this refinance available: non-credit qualifying and credit qualifying.

HUD: A form used by a settlement or closing agent itemizing all charges imposed on a borrower and seller in a real estate transaction. This form gives a picture of the closing transaction, and provides each party with a complete list of incoming and outgoing funds. "Buyers" are referred to as "borrowers" on this form even if no loan is involved.

Mortgage derivative: Mortgage derivatives are investment securities developed by the financial industry to provide different risk and interest-rate profiles from pools of mortgages.

Negative amortization (NegAm): An increase in the principal balance of a loan caused by making payments that fail to cover the interest due. The remaining amount of interest owed is added to the loan's principal, which ultimately causes the borrower to owe more money.

Option adjustable-rate mortgages (ARMs): A type of mortgage where the mortgagor (borrower) has several options as to which type of payment is made to the mortgagee (lender). In addition to having the choice of making payments of interest and principal that amounts to those made in conventional mortgages, option ARMs also have alternative payment options where the mortgagor can make significantly smaller payments by making interest-only payments or minimum payments.

Series 66: The Series 66 is a combination of the Series 65 (Investment Advisor Exam) and the Series 63 (Uniform State Law Agent Exam). This section focuses on the skills and knowledge needed by an Investment Advisor (IA) to provide investment advice to clients. The Series 66 tests your ability to understand the concept of the time value of money, as well as the different measures of potential rates of return.

Series 7: A general securities registered representative license administered by the Financial Industry Regulatory Authority (FINRA) that entitles the holder to sell all types of securities products with the exception of commodities and futures.

Teaser rate: An initial rate on an adjustable-rate mortgage (ARM). This rate will typically be below the going market rate, and is used by lenders to entice borrowers to choose ARMs over traditional mortgages. The teaser rate will be in effect for only a few months, at which point the rate will gradually climb until it reaches the full indexed rate, which will be a static margin rate plus the floating rate index to which the mortgage is tied (usually the LIBOR index).

United States Department of Agriculture (USDA): A department of the United States government that manages various programs related to food, agriculture, natural resources, rural development and nutrition. The United States Department of Agriculture tries to expand economic opportunity in rural areas, make sure Americans are properly fed and conserve natural resources. President Lincoln founded the USDA in 1862, at a time when about 50% of Americans lived on farms.

VA Interest Rate Reduction Refinance Loans (IRRRLs): A mortgage refinancing program offered by the U.S. Department of Veterans Affairs (VA) to homeowners with VA loans. The VA Interest Rate Reduction Refinance Loan (IRRRL) is a VA-loan-to-VA-loan process, designed to allow homeowners to refinance a fixed loan at a lower interest rate or to convert an adjustable rate mortgage (ARM) into a fixed rate mortgage.

Yield Spread Premium (YSP): A form of compensation that a mortgage broker, acting as the intermediary, receives from the original lender for selling an interest rate to a borrower that is above the lender's par rate for which the borrower qualifies. The yield spread premium must be disclosed on the HUD-1 Form when the loan is closed.

All definitions brought to you by Investopedia.

About the Authors

Jason C. Myers has been in the mortgage industry since 2002 and was featured on the Inc. 5000, a list of the fastest-growing private companies in the nation, in 2012 & 2013. He lives in Charleston, South Carolina, with his wife, two children, and golden retriever.

Michael Shannon II graduated from The Kelley School of Business at Indiana University – Indianapolis and moved to Charleston, South Carolina. He has been working in both finance and marketing since 2008 and started working with Jason in June of 2014.

For all the updates on mortgage products, my upcoming books, and to be on my VIP email list with exclusive newsletters, check me out at www.JasonCMyers.com or email me directly at Info@JasonCMyers.com.

66514800R00090

Made in the USA
San Bernardino, CA
12 January 2018